WISDOM OF THE EAST

THE DIWAN OF ZEB-UN-NISSA

WISDOM OF THE EAST

THE DIWAN OF ZEB-UN-NISSA

THE FIRST FIFTY GHAZALS

RENDERED FROM THE PERSIAN BY

MAGAN LAL

AND

JESSIE DUNCAN WESTBROOK

WITH AN INTRODUCTION AND NOTES

GYAN

Published by

GYAN

Gyan Publishing House
5, Ansari Road
Daryaganj, New Delhi-110002
Phone: 011-47034999, 9811692060
E-mail: books@gyanbooks.com

Distribution Network
gyanbooks.com
India, USA, Canada, UK, Australia, France

ISBN : 978-81-212-2303-4 (PB)
First Published, 1913

2nd Impression 2021

Printed at: Gyan Press, Delhi.

Wisdom of the East
The Diwan of ZEB-UN-Nissa
Author: Magan Lal and Jessie Duncan Westbrook

WISDOM OF THE EAST

THE DIWAN OF ZEB-UN-NISSA

THE FIRST FIFTY GHAZALS

RENDERED FROM THE PERSIAN BY

MAGAN LAL

AND

JESSIE DUNCAN WESTBROOK

WITH AN INTRODUCTION AND NOTES

LONDON

JOHN MURRAY, ALBEMARLE STREET, W.

1913

CONTENTS

Thy pleasaunce, Princess, now is desolate;
Where once the gleaming water-courses traced
Their paths among the cypresses, a waste
Stretches beyond thy ruined garden-gate;
The rose is dead, the bulbul flown away,
And Zeb-un-Nissa but a memory.

But where the rapt faquirs God's praises tell,
Where at the shrine the pious pilgrims meet,
Thy verses, Makhfi, holy tongues repeat,
Thy name is honoured and remembered well:
For through thy words they win a fleeting gleam
Of the Divine Belovèd of their dream.

So might we, even in an alien tongue,
Bring from thy mystic garden, where, apart,
Thou dwelt communing with thy burning heart,
These echoes of the songs that thou hast sung,
And catch thy vision of the Soul's Desire,
The immortal Phœnix with its wings of fire.

J. D. W.

INTRODUCTION

THE Princess Zeb-un-Nissa was the eldest daughter of the Mogul Emperor Aurungzebe of India, and was born in 1639. She came of a distinguished line, in direct descent from Genghiz Khan and Tamerlane. Her Emperor-ancestors were famous not only for their valour and statesmanship, but as patrons and inspirers of art and learning, and, moreover, they themselves possessed distinguished literary gifts. Baber's reminiscences are written in so fresh and delightful a style that their charm holds us to-day, and he wrote poetry both in Turki and Persian, even inventing a new style of verse. One of his sons, Mirza Kamran, was also a writer of Persian verse. Although Akbar has given the world no writings of his own—tradition even says that he never found time to learn to write—yet he surrounded himself with a most cultured circle; and Abul Fazl, his talented minister, constantly records in his letters Akbar's wise sayings and noble sentiments. Jehangir, like Baber, wrote his own memoirs, and they are ranked high in Persian literature. Shah Jehan wrote some account of his court and of his travels, and a record called the Dastur-ul-Amal, or Laws of Shah Jehan. Aurungzebe wrote books on Musulman law, and the collection of his letters, called the Ruqat Alamgiri, is famous. Nor was this literary talent confined to the men's side of the house. Baber's daughter, Gulbadan, wrote some history of her own times, and has left us an interesting picture of Baber himself; and Zeb-un-Nissa's verses still testify to her skill as a poet.

It is difficult to learn precisely the details of her life; they were not written in any connected biography, for in her later days she incurred the wrath of her stern father, and no court chronicler dared to speak of her. Her mother was Dilrus Banu Begum, daughter of Shah Nawaz Khan. From her childhood she showed great intelligence, and she was instructed from an early age. At seven years old she was a Hafiz—she knew the Koran by heart; and her father gave a great feast to celebrate the occasion. We read that the whole army was feasted in the great Maidan at Delhi, thirty thousand gold mohurs were given to the poor, and the public offices were closed for two days. She was given as teacher a lady named Miyabai, and learned Arabic in four years; she then studied mathematics and astronomy, in which sciences she gained rapid proficiency. She began to write a commentary on the Koran, but this was stopped by her father. From her early youth she wrote verses, at first in Arabic; but when an Arabian scholar saw her work he said: "Whoever has written this poem is Indian. The verses are clever and wise, but the idiom is Indian, although it is a miracle for a foreigner to know Arabian so well." This piqued her desire for perfection, and thereafter she wrote in Persian, her mother-tongue. She had as tutor a scholar called Shah Rustum Ghazi, who encouraged and directed her literary tastes. She wrote at first in secret, but he found copies of her verses among her exercise-books. He prophesied her future greatness, and persuaded her father to send all over India and Persia and Kashmir to find poets and to invite them to come to Delhi to form a fitting circle for the princess. This was the more wonderful as Aurungzebe himself cared little for poetry and used to speak against the poet's calling. He had forbidden the works of Hafiz to be read in school by boys, or in the palace by the Begums, but he made an exception in favour of Zeb-un-Nissa.

Among the poets of her circle were Nasir Ali, Sayab, Shamsh Wali Ullah, Brahmin, and Behraaz. Nasir Ali came from Sirhind, and was famous for his pride and his poverty, for he despised the protection of the great. Zeb-un-Nissa admired his verses, and in a way he came to be regarded almost as her rival poet. Her coterie used to engage in a poetical tournament—a kind of war of wits. One would propose a line—sometimes it would be a question ; another would answer it or contradict it or qualify it or expand it, by a line or lines in the same metre, rhyming with the original line. This is called *mushaira*—a poetical concourse ; and in this quick repartee Zeb-un-Nissa excelled.

She had been betrothed by the wish of Shah Jehan, her grandfather, to Suleiman Shikoh, who was her cousin and son of Dara Shikoh ; but Aurungzebe, who hated and feared Dara, was unwilling that the marriage should take place, and caused the young prince to be poisoned. She had many other suitors for her hand, but she demanded that she should see the princes and test their attainments before a match was arranged. One of those who wished to marry her was Mirza Farukh, son of Shah Abbas II of Iran ; she wrote to him to come to Delhi so that she might see what he was like. The record remains of how he came with a splendid retinue, and was feasted by Zeb-un-Nissa in a pleasure-house in her garden, while she waited on him with her veil upon her face. He asked for a certain sweetmeat in words which, by a play of language, also meant a kiss, and Zeb-un-Nissa, affronted, said: "Ask for what you want from our kitchen." She told her father that, in spite of the prince's beauty and rank, his bearing did not please her, and she refused the marriage. Mirza Farukh, however, sent her this verse: "I am determined never to leave this temple; here will I bow my head, here will I prostrate myself, here will I serve, and here alone is happiness." Zeb-un-Nissa answered: "How light dost thou esteem this game of love, O child. Nothing dost thou know of the fever of longing, and the fire of separation, and the burning flame of love." And so he returned to Persia without her.

She enjoyed a great deal of liberty in the palace: she wrote to many learned men of her time, and held discussions with them. She was a great favourite with her uncle Dara Shikoh, who was a scholar and wide-minded and enlightened. To him she modestly attributed her verses when first she began to write, and many of the ghazals in the Diwan of Dara Shikoh are by her. She came out in the court, and helped in her father's councils, but always with the veil upon her face. Perhaps she liked the metaphor of the face hidden till the day when the Divine Belovèd should come; perhaps life behind carven lattices had a charm for her; for her pen-name is Makhfi, the hidden one. Once Nasir Ali said this verse: "O envy of the moon, lift up thy veil and let me enjoy the wonder of thy beauty." She answered:—

I will not lift my veil,—
For, if I did, who knows?
The bulbul might forget the rose,
The Brahman worshipper
Adoring Lakshmi's grace
Might turn, forsaking her,
To see my face;
My beauty might prevail.
Think how within the flower
Hidden as in a bower
Her fragrant soul must be,
And none can look on it;
So me the world can see
Only within the verses I have writ—
I will not lift the veil.

She was deeply religious, but she was a Sufi, and did not share her father's cold and narrow orthodoxy. One day she was walking in the garden, and, moved by the beauty of the world around her, exclaimed, "Four things are necessary to make me happy—wine and flowers and a running stream and the face of the Belovèd." Again and again she recited the couplet; suddenly she came upon Aurungzebe, on a marble platform under a tree close by, wrapt in meditation. She was seized with fear, thinking he might have heard her profane words; but, as if she had not noticed him, she went on chanting as before, but with the second line changed, "Four things are necessary for happiness—prayers and fasting and tears and repentance!"

She belonged, like her father, to the Sunni sect of Musulmans, and was well versed in controversial religious points. One of Aurungzebe's sons, Muhammad Ma'uzam, was a Shiah, and when sectarian disputes took place in the court the princess was often asked to settle them. Her decision in one dispute is famous, for it was copied and sent to Iran and Turan, and many scores of Begums are said to have been converted to the Sunni cause on that occasion. At first she took great pleasure in the Tazia celebrations, but gave them up at her father's wish when he came to the throne, and adopted a simpler form of faith.

Much of her personal allowance of four lakhs a year she used in encouraging men of letters, in providing for widows and orphans, and in sending every year pilgrims to Mecca and Medina. She collected a fine library and employed skilled caligraphers to copy rare and valuable books for her; and, as Kashmir paper and Kashmir scribes were famous for their excellence, she had a scriptorium also in that province, where work went on constantly. Her personal interest in the work was great, and every morning she went over the copies that had been made on the previous day. She had contemporary fame as a poet, and literary men used to send their works for her approval or criticism, and she rewarded them according to their merits.

In personal appearance she is described as

being tall and slim, her face round and fair in colour, with two moles, or beauty-spots, on her left cheek. Her eyes and abundant hair were very black, and she had thin lips and small teeth. In Lahore Museum is a contemporary portrait, which corresponds to this description. She did not use missia for blackening between the teeth, nor antimony for darkening her eyelashes, though this was the fashion of her time. Her voice was so beautiful that when she read the Koran she moved her hearers to tears. In dress she was simple and austere; in later life she always wore white, and her only ornament was a string of pearls round her neck. She is held to have invented a woman's garment, the angya kurti, a modification, to suit Indian conditions, of the dress of the women of Turkestan; it is now worn all over India. She was humble in her bearing, courteous, patient, and philosophic in enduring trouble; no one, it is said, ever saw her with a ruffled forehead. Her chief friend was a girl named Imami, a poet like herself. Zeb-un-Nissa was skilled in the use of arms, and several times took part in war.

In the beginning of 1662 Aurungzebe was taken ill, and, his physicians prescribing change of air, he took his family and court with him to Lahore. At that time Akil Khan, the son of his vizier, was governor of that city. He was famous for his beauty and bravery, and was also a poet. He had heard of Zeb-un-Nissa, and knew her verses, and was anxious to see her. On pretence of guarding the city, he used to ride round the walls of the palace, hoping to catch a glimpse of her. One day he was fortunate; he caught sight of her on the house-top at dawn, dressed in a robe of gulnar, the colour of the flower of the pomegranate. He said, "A vision in red appears on the roof of the palace." She heard and answered, completing the couplet: "Supplications nor force nor gold can win her." She liked Lahore as a residence, and was laying out a garden there: one day Akil Khan heard that she had gone with her companions to see a marble pavilion which was being built in it. He disguised himself as a mason, and, carrying a hod, managed to pass the guards and enter. She was playing chausar with some of her girl friends, and he, passing near, said: "In my longing for thee I have become as the dust wandering round the earth." She understood and answered immediately: "Even if thou hadst become as the wind, thou shouldst not touch a tress of my hair." They met again and again, but some rumour reached the ears of Aurungzebe, who was at Delhi, and he hastened back. He wished to hush up the matter by hurrying her into marriage at once. Zeb-un-Nissa demanded freedom of choice, and asked that portraits of her suitors should be sent to her; and chose naturally that of Akil Khan. Aurungzebe sent for him; but a disappointed rival wrote to him: "It is no child's play to be the lover of a daughter of a king. Aurungzebe knows your doings; as soon as you come to Delhi, you will reap the fruit of your love." Akil Khan thought the Emperor planned revenge. So, alas for poor Zeb-un-Nissa! at the critical moment her lover proved a coward; he declined the marriage, and wrote to the king resigning his service. Zeb-un-Nissa was scornful and disappointed, and wrote: "I hear that Akil Khan has left off paying homage to me"—or the words might also mean, "has resigned service"—"on account of some foolishness." He answered, also in verse, "Why should a wise man do that which he knows he will regret?" (Akil also means, a wise man). But he came secretly to Delhi to see her again, perhaps regretting his fears. Again they met in her garden; the Emperor was told and came unexpectedly, and Zeb-un-Nissa, taken unawares, could think of no hiding-place for her lover but a deg, or large cooking-vessel. The Emperor asked, "What is in the deg?" and was answered, "Only water to be heated." "Put it on the fire, then," he ordered; and it was done. Zeb-un-Nissa at that moment thought more of her reputation than of her lover, and came near the deg and whispered, "Keep silence if you are my true lover, for the sake of my honour." One of her verses says, "What is the fate of a lover? It is to be crucified for the world's pleasure." One wonders if she thought of Akil Khan's sacrifice of his life.

After this she was imprisoned in the fortress of Salimgarh, some say because her father distrusted her on account of her friendship with her brother, Prince Akbar, who had revolted against him; others say because of her sympathy with the Mahratta chieftain Sivaji. There she spent long years, and there she wrote much bitter poetry:—

So long these fetters cling to my feet! My friends have become enemies, my relations are strangers to me.

What more have I to do with being anxious to keep my name undishonoured when friends seek to disgrace me?

Seek not relief from the prison of grief, O Makhfi; thy release is not politic.

O Makhfi, no hope of release hast thou until the Day of Judgment come.

Even from the grave of Majnun the voice comes to my ears—"O Leila, there is no rest for the victim of love even in the grave."

I have spent all my life, and I have won nothing but sorrow, repentance, and the tears of unfulfilled desire:—

Long is thine exile, Makhfi, long thy yearning,
Long shalt thou wait, thy heart within thee burning,
Looking thus forward to thy home-returning.
But now what home hast thou, unfortunate ?
The years have passed and left it desolate,
The dust of ages blows across its gate.

If on the Day of Reckoning
God say, "In due proportion I will pay
And recompense thee for thy suffering,"
Lo, all the joys of heaven it would outweigh;
Were all God's blessings poured upon me, yet
He would be in my debt.

When her memory was becoming dim in the hearts of her friends, Nasir Ali alone thought of her, and wrote a poem to her, saying that, now, the world could not delight in her presence, and he himself had to go about the earth unhappy, having no one but himself to appreciate his verses. But she sent no answering word.

When she was released she lived solitary in Delhi, and the verses she wrote there are very melancholy, telling of the faithlessness of the times :—

Why shouldst thou, O Makhfi, complain of friends, or even of enemies ? Fate has frowned upon thee from the beginning of time.

Let no one know the secrets of thy love. On the way of love, O Makhfi, walk alone. Even if Jesus seek to be thy companion, tell him thou desirest not his comradeship.

Here is one of her saddest poems, expressing something of the tragedy of her life :—

O idle arms,
Never the lost Beloved have ye caressed:
Better that ye were broken than like this
Empty and cold eternally to rest.

O useless eyes,
Never the lost Beloved for all these years
Have ye beheld: better that ye were blind
Than dimmed thus by my unavailing tears.

O foolish springs,
That bring not the Beloved to my abode;
Yea, all the friends of youth have gone from me,
Each has set out on his appointed road.

O fading rose,
Dying unseen as hidden thou wert born;
So my heart's blossom fallen in the dust
Was ne'er ordained His turban to adorn.

She died in 1689 after seven days' illness, and was buried in her garden at Nawakot, near Lahore, according to the instructions she left. The tomb is desolate now, although once it was made of fine marbles, and had over its dome a pinnacle of gold; it was ruined in the troublous times of the dissolution of the Mogul Empire. The great gate still stands, large enough for an elephant with a howdah to enter, and within the enclosure is a tower with four minarets, roofed with turquoise and straw-yellow tiles. But the garden that was in its time very splendid, being held second only to that of the Shalimar of Shah Jehan, has disappeared; and the walls rise up now from the waving fields of grain.

The garden which she laid out in Lahore itself and which was called the Chauburgi, or four-towered, can still be traced by portions of the walls and gates remaining. Three of the turrets over the archway still stand, ornamented with tiles in patterns of cypress-trees and growing flowers, and the gateways have inscriptions in Arabic and Persian. One of these tells that she presented the garden to her old instructress Miyabai.

In 1724, thirty-five years after her death, what could be found of her scattered writings were collected under the name of the *Diwan-i-Makhfi*, literally, the Book of the Hidden One. It contained four hundred and twenty-one ghazals and several rubais. In 1730 other ghazals were added. Many manuscript copies were made in both India and Persia; some beautifully illuminated examples are known and preserved.

The *Diwan-i-Makhfi* shares the characteristics of other Sufic poetry—the worship of God under the form of the Beautiful Belovèd, who is adorable but tyrannical, who reduces the lover to abject despair, but at last bestows on him a gleam of hope when he is at the point of death. The Belovèd is the Hunter of the Soul, chasing it like a deer through the jungle of the world:—

I have no peace, the quarry I, a Hunter chases me,
It is Thy memory;
I turn to flee, but fall; for over me he casts his snare,
Thy perfumed hair.
Who can escape Thy prison? no mortal heart is free
From dreams of Thee.

The lover is the madman, who for his love is scorned and mocked by the unsympathetic world. The personified Power of Evil, the Enemy, lurks at the devotee's elbow, ready to distract him from the contemplation of God.

The poet was evidently acquainted, not only with the theories of Sufism, but with the practices of the faquirs as well. We read of the assembly of the devout, as in the Dargah at Ajmer to-day: how they greet the morning with floods of tears and deep sighs, how they beat their hearts of stone till the sparks of divine love fly out from them. The hatchet to strike the flinty heart is the symbol of the Sufic poet: one sees it in the portraits of Hafiz and others. There is also the scoffing at the orthodox who meet within the mosque, and the glorification of the more advanced soul to whom all the universe is the temple of God, nay even God himself —"Where I make my prayer—at that place is the Kiblah."

But the poems of Zeb-un-Nissa, in addition to what they share with other Sufic poetry, have a special Indian flavour of their own. She inherited the Akbar tradition of the unification of religions, and knew not only Islam, but Hinduism and Zoroastrianism also. Her special triumph consists in that she weaves together the religious traditions and harmonizes them with Sufic practices. In some of her poems she hails the sun as the symbol of deity. Constantly she speaks of the mosque and the temple together or antithetically—saying that God is equally in both, or too great to be worshipped in either :—

No Muslim I,
But an idolater,
I bow before the image of my Love,
And worship her :

No Brahman I,
My sacred thread
I cast away, for round my neck I wear
Her plaited hair instead.

Sometimes she even combines the Hindu and Musulman idea :

In the mosque I seek my idol-shrine.

On the Day of Judgment we should have had much difficulty in proving that we were true believers, had we not brought with us our belovèd Kafir idol as a witness.

The glorification or adoration of the *pir*, or spiritual teacher, is also shown in her poems. He is the intermediary between God and man, and is sometimes symbolized as the Morning Breeze, bringing from the enclosed garden the fragrance to those, less privileged, who can only stand without the gate.

The *Diwan-i-Makhfi* is widely read in India, and is highly esteemed. Its verse is chanted in the ecstatic concourses which meet at festivals at the tombs of celebrated saints; so that, although her tomb has been despoiled of the splendour which befitted the resting-place of a Mogul princess, she has the immortality she perhaps would have desired. In one of her verses she says:—I am the daughter of a King, but I have taken the path of renunciation, and this is my glory, as my name Zeb-un-Nissa, being interpreted, means that I am the glory of womankind.

J. D. W.

DULWICH VILLAGE,
March 1913.

بسم الله الرحمن الرحیم

In the Name of God, the Compassionate, the Merciful

THE DIWAN OF ZEB-UN-NISSA

I

To Thee, first,
From the clouds of Whose mercy is born
The rose of my garden, I look!
Let the praise of Thy love the beginning adorn
Of the verse of my book.

Athirst
For Thy love are my body and soul;
Like Mansur the grains of this clod,
My body, cry out—They are parts, Thou the whole,
Themselves they are God.

The waves
Of Thy deluge of love o'er the boat
Of mortality roll;
No Noah could lift from the deeps till it float
My love-drownèd soul.

As slaves
The powers of the darkness for me
Will obedient fly;
If a word of my praise be accepted by Thee,
Like Suleiman I.

And now
No more do the ready tears start
As laments from my tongue,
For like pearls the blood-drops that are drawn from my heart
On my lashes are hung.

Bear thou,
O Makhfi, with patience thy pain,
It is endless, and leave thou the night
Of thy passions; for then shall not Khizr attain
Such a spring of delight.

II

O Thou Who all things mortal and divine
Hast fashioned, and by Whom alone we live,
May there still shine
The torch of hope that Thou to us didst give!

Within us stirs the leaven of Thy love,
As streams of water of Thy mercy run.
Look from above
And bless Mahmoud and all that he hath done.

Whether it be in Mecca's holiest shrine,
Or in the Temple pilgrim feet have trod,
Still Thou art mine,
Wherever God is worshipped is my God.

The morning I shall greet with tears and sighs,
And from my heart that burns with holy fire
A breath shall rise
To burnish thus my mirror of desire.

Give me thy tears, O Makhfi, let them rain
In quenching torrents on my burning heart;
So hot its pain
At every sigh I breathe the flames outstart.

III

O Prophet, o'er the world
Thy soul-compelling banner is unfurled:
See how thy faith hath spread
Till Iran and Arabia are led.
Thy lips unclose
Like petals of a newly-budded rose,
And from them flow
Thy words of wisdom, till not only know
The sons of men,
But birds within the garden sing again
Thy words of gold.
O thou whose beauty I with joy behold,
Nature in truth
Made never loveliness like to thy youth.
Snared me it hath
Till fain would I renunciation's path
With patience tread,
And follow where thy holy feet have led.
But how can I
My cherished joys to my poor heart deny,
Or, even more,
My cherished sorrows can I yield, for sore
My heart doth bleed
Where cruel love hath wounded it indeed.

Look thou and see
Where from my wounds there drops continually
A crimson flood;
But fragrant flowers are springing from my blood,
And every thorn
Wherewith my weary wandering feet are torn
Turns to a rose.
O Makhfi, if the Kaaba keeper close
To thee his door,
Complain not: thou possessest even more
A holy place;
For look into the Well-Belovèd Face,
Over His Eyes
Arches more fair than Kaaba gates arise;
Thy heart shall bend,
Itself an archway welcoming the Friend.

IV

My eager heart a pang of rapture stings
  When the long-wandering wind unto me brings
    The perfume of thy presence on its wings.

And so I wait in this my sorrow's night,
  Until thou givest to my weary sight
    Thy beauty for my longing eyes' delight.

The world through Islam light in darkness saw
  And walked safe guided by thy Scroll of Law,
    Bowing to God in hope and holy awe—

To God, Who sinners can forgive and lead,
  Inscrutable Himself, yet Who can read
    The hidden heart and comprehend its need.

O Prophet, shining like a lonely gem,
  The fairest of Heaven's highest diadem,
    Look on men's need and intercede for them.

Thou art the veil through which the light doth
    shine,
  Nay, thou thyself the very torch divine—
    Naught else behold these dazzled eyes of mine.

V

HERE is the path of love—how dark and long
  Its winding ways, with many snares beset!
Yet crowds of eager pilgrims onward throng
  And fall like doves into the fowler's net.

Now tell me what the grain that drew the dove?
  The mole it was upon a cheek so fair.
Tell me of what was wove the net of love?
  The wandering curls of the Belovèd's hair.

The festival of love is holden here,
  The goblet passes; drink thou of this wine,
Yea, drain it to the lees, and never fear
  Intoxication that is all divine.

How easy 'tis to sigh and to complain!
  All the world weeps to give its woe relief;
But proudly in thy heart conceal thy pain,
  And silent drink the poison of thy grief.

Here is the source of light, the heavenly fount,
  Here is the vision of eternal grace;
Brighter than Moses thou, when from the Mount
  He came, God's radiance shining in his face.

The wine at night unto the morning lends
  Its exaltation, morning to the night
Its dream bequeaths in turn: so never ends
  The sequence of the happy soul's delight.

But, Makhfi, tell me where the feast is made?
  Where are the merry-makers? Lo, apart,
Here in my soul the feast of God is laid,
  Within the hidden chambers of my heart.

VI

My heart is looted of its treasure, left
Careless and unprotected, to my shame,
And thus I weep, feeling myself bereft,
Knowing myself to blame.

With mine own hands the altar-fire I lit;
As flame within a lamp my heart afire
Glows even through the body casing it,
And burns it with desire.

Could I my foolish heart to ashes burn
Then might I rest, my sorrow then might cease;
Unto the ocean of Thy love I turn
To find within it peace.

I sink within its waters, nor above
Its surface can my weary limbs uplift,
Deep-drownèd I within the sea of love
Lapped by its waves must drift.

A wilderness this lonely heart of mine
Till love transformed it to another guise,
And now it shines as fair as the divine
Gardens of Paradise.

I would that I my longing might outpour,
My grief might turn to hymns, my pain might tell
In psalms like that sweet singer sang of yore,
David of Israel.

Unto the fields like pecking birds I go
To gather up the ears of golden grain,
But only tears, not corn, I gather—lo,
They fall in floods like rain.

O wise one, at the feast of love be glad,
But careful too, and guard thy cup of wine;
In ecstasy I drank the share I had,
O Sage, take heed of thine.

With slumber, Makhfi, heavy are thine eyes,
And though thy tale has not attained its close,
So deep a languor on thy spirit lies;
Seek thou for it repose.

VII

As at the coming of the spring-tide rains
Rivers of sap through growing trees upstart,
So runs Thy love throughout my very veins,
Yea, to the tender tendrils of my heart.

I beat my flinty heart till from it flies
The spark divine of the eternal fire,
And from the flashing gleams I see arise
The lightning of Thy love—my heart's desire.

Come, O ye weak in faith, for help is here,
Behold these flashes from our hearts that fly,
Had ye the eye of faith they would appear
Like the white light that gleamed on Sinai.

Come to the feast of love, for it is spread;
Share ye the wine-cup where we drink so deep;
Behold the wine—the tears that we have shed,
The wine-cups are our eyes that ever weep.

But, as we drink, upon us falls the spell,
The dream, the vision, and the ecstasy;
The wine of pain turns blood, nor can we tell
If we exist, or if we cease to be.

Within the jungle of this world of woe
The lion of desire stalks ravenous.
Girded with faith let us as hunters go:
If we resist him he will flee from us.

Ofttimes my heart can sing and can rejoice,
Pouring forth hymns throughout my rapturous
days;
Alas, that powers of evil choke my voice,
And blast my thoughts, and burn my psalms of
praise!

VIII

From the glance Thou bestowed, O Belovèd,
flows beauty no words can express;
My life—it were little to offer in thanks for Thy
bountifulness.
How shamed were the pious assembly, how
grieved in their hearts when they heard
That for love of Thy fluttering tresses the utter-
most nations were stirred.
My heart is riven in fragments, ravaged by tears
of my grief,
But to one whom Thy lashes have wounded never
there cometh relief.
At Thy feet, O haughty Belovèd, I lay down the
pride of my brow,
I am near to Thy heart as Thy raiment; why
sayest "A stranger art thou"?
O Makhfi, walk boldly like Majnun in the valley
of grief undismayed,
Girt round with thy new dedication, the promise
of love thou hast made.

IX

O Saki, do thy task;
Into this moon-like goblet pour
The golden wine that, shining like the sun,
From out the dusky flask
Comes till my goblet bubbles o'er,
As from the clouds the dawn when night is done.

Behold my luckless heart,
So broken, so dissolved by pain,
It even flows in tears between my lashes;
And yet how can I part
With it, while still to me remain
Its shards—I wait till it is burnt to ashes.

I knew long, long ago,
Your promises were less than naught,
I blotted them for ever from my mind.
Why was I born to know
An age above all others fraught
With love ungrateful and with fate unkind?

But grasp thy joy; who knows,
Makhfi, what may to thee befall?
The firm foundations of the earth may shake,
The breeze that blows
May, if this empty life be all,
The bubble of our vain existence break.

X

I ASK not from Heaven that it give
Fortune or power,
I ask but a garden apart,
Where for the brief hour
That we are appointed to live,
Of earth the delight that is nearest divine
Might be mine—
To live in the love of the friends of my heart.

The rapturous nightingale sings,
Wooing the rose
In the midst of the garden new-born:
But only the gardener knows
Of the labour that brings
To the garden its beauty; he toiled in the heat,
And his feet
Have been wounded by many a thorn.

Immortal is beauty, for, see,
Like the sun in his might,
It illumines the worlds and all things that are made
With the joy of its light;
For this be our thanks unto Thee,

And for the great teachers vouchsafed in our need
To guide and to lead,
Their presence to be our safe shelter and shade.

Upon us Thy mercy bestow!
Consider how weak,
How afflicted we are and how sorrowful; then
When we passionate seek
For oblivion, and Thou dost know
How time on our desolate spirit has beat
And brought us defeat—
O save us, nor let us endure it again.

O happy the seer who knows
Good and evil are one,
Who has learned how self-poised he may live,
Who is shaken by none,
To whom spring with its rose
And autumn are equal:—not him canst thou teach
Or, careless one, preach
To him; thou indeed hast no counsel to give.

If perilous love doth thee lead,
If thou enter his track,
In the desert like Majnun thou dwell'st evermore,
Thou shalt never look back;
Nor even take heed

To thy life if thou lose it or keep it, and pain
Shalt disdain,
Nor seek on the limitless ocean of love for a shore.

O Makhfi, as out of the nest
The fledgling birds fall
And fluttering, helpless, are caught in the snares,
So see after all
Thou art caught like the rest,
For, flying too boldly, thy feeble wings fail,
And thou dost bewail
Thy fate, thus enmeshed in the net of thy cares.

XI

Awake, arise, my soul, for it is spring;
  Let the narcissus, with its scent divine,
Cast its bewitchment, let the Saki bring
  His idol, for indeed he worships wine.

To the forbidden path turn not aside,
  And, tyrannous Belovèd, let thine eye
Look on thy victims trampled in thy pride,
  Who for a glance from thee would gladly die.

Some pay their worship at the Kaaba shrine,
  Some pray within the Temple courts apart,
But, Makhfi, think what secret joy is thine,
  To bear thine idol ever in thy heart.

XII

FRIENDS had I, many friends, who shared with me
Days glad and sad,
But mine they are no more, I am cut free
From all I had.

Dust falls within the cup of Kaikobad
And King Jamshid,
Nor recks the world if they were sad or glad,
Or what they did.

Only to-day have we, and through the sand,
With feet that tire,
We march, but never reach the promised land
Of heart's desire.

I follow on where Wisdom's feet have led,
And firmly hold,
The while this hard and thorny path I tread,
Her garment's fold.

How many hearts, O Love, thy sword hath slain,
And yet will slay!
They bless thee, nor to God will they complain
At Judgment Day.

When in the mosque to seek thine idol there
Thou wendest, may
Thy steps fall gently, Makhfi, lest thou scare
The birds away.

XIII

Why should I argue that on Sinai
Celestial radiance glows?
I cannot reason; though the world deny,
My heart enlightened knows.

My heart is hot within me, yea, has burst
In flames of love the while
So fierce that like a drop to slake my thirst
Were all the floods of Nile.

So deep in sin am I—I cannot wend
Where holy pilgrims fare
To Mecca, even if Abraham, God's friend,
Should come to lead me there.

I tire of wisdom's kingdom which is mine,
I tire of reason's sway:
Passion of love, O carry me to thine,
A hundred miles away.

Lo, when I come unto the water's side
The obedient waves retire,
My flaming heart exultantly shall guide
Like Moses' torch of fire.

Though evil days are mine, of joy bereft,
    With pain that never ends,
Fate, do with me your worst, there still is left
    The Friend beyond all friends.

Tell me, O Makhfi, is it I who sin ?
    Is this my sin I bear ?
Is it the body's or the soul's within
    That lived and sinned elsewhere ?

XIV

O FOOLISH heart,
Thy carelessness how can I comprehend?
Hast thou no strength, no will, to tear apart
The barrier that divides me from my Friend?

See how the budding flower,
Emerging fair from out her torn green dress,
Is beauteous in the garden for her hour,
As Yusuf in his youthful loveliness.

Go, breeze of spring,
Haste to tell Yakub, blinded by his tears,
The tidings that shall end his sorrowing
And lift the darkness from his troubled years.

Treading love's path so long,
Under such heavy burdens did I bow,
At last my chastened heart has grown so strong,
No task, no pain, can bend my spirit now.

O fortunate,
More blessed than Alexander's lot is mine.
Come to me, O ye thirsty: this my fate—
To know the giver of celestial wine.

I have wiped clean my heart
From actions, yea, and from desires as well,
And yearn alone for peace, to have no part
At Judgment Day, either in Heaven or Hell.

XV

Behold the fire renewed within my heart,
My sighs have lashed it with their breath until
the flames outstart;
Nor may this feeble cage, my body, stay
The fluttering of this bird, my soul, that longs to
fly away.
The rocks would melt, and into tears would
flow,
Could they but hear the never-ending murmur
of my woe;
For in the dark foreboding of my heart
There sounds the warning bell that calls the
caravan to start:
O Love, I have bewailed for all these years
Thy tyranny, but none has heard my voice
except my tears.
Behold how poor I am, but yet so proud,
I would not sit at Hatim's table with the eager
crowd:
See, I have watched throughout the lonely
night
Of separation, when there never came my heart's
delight,

And in my desolation tears of blood
Gushed from my stricken, widowed heart in never-ending flood:
Yet to me, purged by grief, does hope arise,
My withered chaplets change to fragrant flowers of Paradise.
Love holds me in these cruel fetters bound,
My faithfulness to Thee: beside Thy feet, a beaten hound,
I crouch and fawn for crumbs of love from Thee.
O Makhfi, if thy sighs could reach the bosom of the sea,
Even within the cold and lightless deep
Caught from thy heart a quenchless flame should leap.

XVI

O Love, I am thy thrall.
As on the tulip's burning petal glows
A spot yet more intense, of deeper dye,
So in my heart a flower of passion blows;
See the dark stain of its intensity,
Deeper than all.

This is my pride—
That I the rose of all the world have sought,
And, still unwearied in the eager quest,
Fainted nor failed have I, and murmured not;
Thus is my head exalted o'er the rest,
My turban glorified.

O blessèd pain,
O precious grief I keep, and sweet unrest,
Desire that dies not, longing past control!
My heart is torn to pieces in my breast,
And for the shining diamond of the soul
I pine in vain.

Behold the light
That from Thy torch of mercy comes to bless
The garden of my heart, Belovèd One,
With the white radiance of its loveliness,
Till my wall's shadow shall outvie the sun,
And seem more bright.

I humbly sit apart;
The Kaaba courts the true believers tread,
I dwell outside, nor mix my praise with theirs;
Yet every fibre of my sacred thread
More precious is to God than all their prayers—
He sees the heart.

O Makhfi sorrowing,
Look from the valley of despair and pain;
The breath of love like morning zephyr blows,
Pearls from thine eyelids fall like gentle rain
Upon the garden, summoning the rose,
Calling the spring.

XVII

The wine of my delight has lost its taste ;
The earth of my existence turns a waste,
No wholesome grass grows there, but only weed ;
My flaming spring of life has passed indeed.
I searched for joy, but never found the end ;
My empty hands, outstretched, can greet no friend ;
And if God's pardon never come to me,
Then less than withered grass my prayers must be.

But, Makhfi, look with a discerning eye—
Deeper than thy despair thy bliss may lie ;
Though on the path of love thy feet may tire,
New strength shall come to thee, and new desire.

XVIII

Tyrannical Love, that goads me and gives me no rest,
As proud as thine arrogant self is this heart in my breast,
It will keep in its pain
Its faithfulness, though it be trampled beneath thy disdain.

This mirror, my heart, is broken against my desire;
O Heaven, give me not of your pity, nay, rather admire
My soul that is proud;
My head, though I beat it in sorrow, has never been bowed.

Think not that with joy and with ease I pursue my desire;
With heart that is weary, with footsteps that lag and that tire,
I follow my quest,
To attain through the difficult way to the kingdom of rest.

Yet, Makhfi, look up from thy desolate region of
night,
And see how the army of sorrow has taken to
flight;
Dawn comes, and despair
Has vanished before the miraculous arrows of
prayer.

XIX

Desolate one, O when
Shalt thou the shining garden see again?
Keep thou within thee, holy and apart,
The garden of thy heart;

As the long-prisoned bird,
Forgetting that it ever flew, and heard
Songs of the wild, and pinions wide unfurled,
Makes of the cage its world.

No fear indeed thou hast,
O heart within the net of love held fast,
Of separation's bitter agony—
Thy love is one with thee.

Sadly we wait and tire,
And sight of the Belovèd Face desire
In vain, till in our hearts the hope is born
Of Resurrection morn.

O heart, thine be no less
Than the ascetic Brahman's faithfulness,
The knotted veins his wasted body bears
As sacred thread he wears.

What is a lover's fate?
What shall befall to him unfortunate?
The world shall cry, to please its idle whim,
"Crucify him!"

Why dost thou then complain
That on thy feet there drags this heavy chain?
Nay, it befits thee well such weights to wear;
Much hast thou learned to bear.

As, far upon the hills,
Despairing Ferhad, weary of life's ills,
Welcomed kind Death, and wept, so for relief
Weep thou and salve thy grief!

And see the thorny waste
Whereon thy bruisèd feet their pathway traced,
This wilderness, touched by thy blood that flows,
Blooms fragrant as the rose.

O Love, shall I repine
The noose of death around my neck to twine
At thy behest? Nay, if thy glory gain,
Proud am I in my pain.

O Makhfi, if thy fate
Be that, without the garden, desolate
Thou dwell—reck not of it; life is a dream,
And we, that seem
To live and move and love, no more at all
Than shadows on a wall.

XX

SAFELY the kings had kept their regal seat,
Nor ever known the poison of defeat,
Had not the Turks the invading army led,
And the crown toppled from each kingly head:
So were we not, O Master, led by thee
Vain were our struggles, scant our victory!

How strong thou hast become, O moth, how great,
Worshipping thus the flame! this is thy fate—
Vainly to love and die, yet thou canst bear
The burning sparks and ever scorn despair:
Thou knowest, fluttering nearer to the fire,
In death thou shalt be one with thy desire.

O cruel Love,—when on the Judgment Day
Thy tyranny God shall in full repay,
And all the blameless blood that thou hast shed
Shall be revenged upon thy haughty head:
Black shall the place of judging be, no less
Than Kerbela's accursèd wilderness.

Haply indeed, O Judge, wilt thou be kind,
And pity in thy heart for sinners find;

Think of the memory of their disgrace,
How dark humiliation stains their face,
The shame that stings and goads them to repent—
Will these not be sufficient punishment ?

Within the desert of the world astray,
How many weary wanderers lose their way !
But Love with beckoning hand appears, to bless,
Finds them a pathway through the wilderness,
And though, like Majnun, in the wild they roam,
Leads them through toils and tribulations home.

XXI

UNTO the garden of attainment ne'er
        Our pathway led,
And never were our eyes anhungered fed
With vision of Thy blessèd countenance,
        Never a glance
Attained we of that face for ever fair.

Wherefor my tears fell down in floods like rain,
        And as I sighed
I thought of my desires unsatisfied,
And memory summoned up with vain regret
        The garden where we met,
But meet no more, I tell my heart with pain.

What have I then to do with high estate?
        Fortune I lay aside
And all wherein the world has taken pride:
Yet in this day of my humility
        Precious to me
As wine of kings I hold my cup of fate.

Despair not, sorrow-laden Makhfi, though
No grass appears
Within this desert watered by thy tears.
Why with their arguing do learnèd men
Question God's mercy, when
His works His infinite compassion show!

XXII

GREEN is my garden, watered by my tears,
And through my soul the perfume of the rose
Kindling my heart with its enchantment flows;
O Saki, bring the cup, for there appears

Gleaming within the garden through the night
A radiance fair our feasting to illume;
What is this glamour shining through the gloom?
My heart's blood, glowing, yields the heavenly light.

O, I have drunk my cup of cherished grief,
And love the torment of my wounded heart;
As the scars heal I tear their lips apart,
And in my pain find rapturous relief.

Why should I then permit the winds of care
To ruffle thus my soul, as airs of spring
Through the Belovèd's tresses wantoning?
For I have risen to fortune from despair.

O fear not, if within the house of prayer
The feeble camphor candle fails and dies;
From out the flaming furnace of my sighs
Will rise another light, more fierce, more fair.

The perfumed winds that with the dawn arise,
  Have they not, Makhfi, caught thy soul away
  And drenched it with delight, so all the day
There cling about thee airs of Paradise ?

XXIII

FOR my love's madness all the world on me
Hath heaped its scorn; so from its ways I flee,
To find a refuge from its cruelty.

A hermitage, with peace my soul to bless,
Here in a corner of the wilderness,
Unseen by secular eyes shall I possess.

Who is the man who boasts to be Love's slave,
And yet this petty life of his would save?
Poor Love, whose votaries are not more brave!

When I was young I asked, and Love gainsaid;
What slips, what wanderings, on Love's road I made,
Until I summoned Wisdom to my aid!

The mirror of my heart I burnish bright
Until, reflected fair for my delight,
The Self's eternal beauty greets my sight.

Like Yaqub blinded by his agony,
No face in all the world is aught to me;
What use have eyes except to look on Thee?

XXIV

How long, O burning heart,
Canst thou keep hidden ! see how flames outstart,
And vapour from thy sighs
Will darken e'en the stars within the skies.
Driven by my love I must
Wander like Majnun, where the desert dust
Falls on his weary head,
Eternally for Leila doomed to shed
His unavailing tears.
The soul by Love enlightened never fears
The unseeing world that says
He must be mad who treads within Love's ways ;
But joyful he and wise,
For Love has given new vision to his eyes.

See, Makhfi, cruel Love,
How in his haughtiness he rides above
The hearts of men, how red
His sword with lovers' blood that he has shed !

XXV

WHEN I behold the garden in the spring,
Rejoicing like a nightingale I sing;
And if the cruel gardener, with his guile,
Try to ensnare me—like a rose I smile.

The morning breeze that from the garden flies
Can give no joy, no gladness, to my eyes;
For, useless breeze, never to me he brings
The fragrance of Thy garments on his wings.

But here before the garden door I wait;
Why should I deem myself unfortunate?
For by Thy holy threshold shall I stay,
And with my lashes sweep its dust away.

This bird, my heart, is taken in Thy net
And flutters unavailingly; but yet,
Thy captive though it be, how canst Thou keep
Prisoned the sighs that from my bosom leap?

O rare and precious Phœnix of the soul,
Vainly I sought for thee; beyond control
My heart has yearned for thee; ever thy wings
Have hung above my soul's imaginings.

Thou Enemy, that hold'st me from my quest,
If even in the sea thou enterest
When from my anger thou dost seek to flee,
My burning soul will find and conquer thee.

O bulbul, glad within the garden sing,
'Tis Makhfi who has won for thee the spring
That blossoms in thy heart ; but in her own
The barren winds of lonely autumn moan.

XXVI

O Love, tell me what is Thy nature, that out of
my kingdom of pride,
Thou canst ravish my soul and canst hold it,
and keep it enslaved at Thy side;
Who knows of Thy infinite wisdom, who knows
what Thy lovers have borne
When madmen the world has proclaimed them
and cast them derision and scorn?

To drink of my blood I am thirsting, to shed it
abroad like a sea,
To sacrifice all am I seeking, to die as a victim
for Thee.
My heart through the anguish of loving has
swooned 'neath the load of its grief,
Come thou with thy magic, O music, and give
to my spirit relief.

Like Ayub I sit in the ashes o'erwhelmed by the
wrath of the skies,
Yet out of the night of my sorrow shall hope
like the morning arise:

To the desolate mountains, like Ferhad, by sorrow
and longing possessed,
I have wandered with pain and with yearning,
with hope and despair in my breast.

Yet, Makhfi, unveiled is thy secret, abroad all
thy passion is told :
Who saw not the beauty of Yusuf when he in
the market was sold ?

XXVII

I HAVE no need for wine :
To me the languorous and magic scent
Breathed by the flowers within the garden, lent
Intoxication that is more divine.

Forgive me then, I pray,
That I no wine in the assembly quaffed,
For I have drunk of a diviner draught,
Its fragrance ever haunts me, night and day.

My heart a bird doth seem
That never joyfully can soar and sing,
For, shut within its cage of sorrowing,
It sees the garden only in a dream.

Shall I not then complain
When every atom of my body cries
Against your tyranny, O cruel skies,
That yield me days so dark and full of pain ?

Grant me, O Fate, this boon,
Give me a little day of joy, of spring,
When even in its cage my heart might sing
Glad as a bird : Death comes, thou knowest, soon.

Although I seem so poor,
Pity me not for empty-handedness;
My haughty eagle soul I still possess,
And I have had the courage to endure.

How many, many years
Within the prison walls of lonely grief
Shall I remain and never know relief,
Like Yaqub, blinded by my useless tears?

Though my proud soul
Torn from its saddle low into the dust
May be by cruel hands of fate downthrust,
I know my feet will somehow reach the goal.

As through life's desert fare
Love's pilgrims, Makhfi, may it be thy pride
Unto Love's realm their caravan to guide,
Thy footsteps be the bell to lead it there.

XXVIII

How uselessly and long I struggled hard
  With thee, mine Enemy, nor from the fight
Aught have I won ; my trait'rous heart I guard,
  And turn away for ever from thy sight.

What wonder if the fire within me rise
  Into a flame outleaping fierce and swift,
And that the heavy vapour of my sighs
  Unto the darkened eyes of Heaven should drift !

Think not, though at the feast no more I sit,
  That I have done with joy : there still remains
The dream that once was mine—I cherish it,
  Like wine its memory courses in my veins.

What though within this valley of Despair
  From sorrow I can never find surcease,
May I be given, in answer to my prayer,
  One day at least of rest, one night of peace !

So sad my fate that, though I long and toil
  Until my forces flag and faint and tire,
I cannot burnish off the stains that soil,
  The rust that dims my mirror of desire.

Though poor I am indeed, yet weak am I
  And cannot dare with my irresolute will
The purse that holds my treasure to untie,
  Its golden harvest in my lap to spill.

And yet, O Makhfi, if with eyes made clear,
  Freed from the world's illusion, thou shalt see,
Lo, the faquir's torn garments shall appear
  More regal than the robes of majesty.

XXIX

IMPATIENT were my hands, and in their haste
Never could they untie the knot of fate,
So vain it is to wail my life laid waste,
        My hours unfortunate.

And strange it is that even in my heart
The sweet tormenting flame of my desire
Is quenched ; impatiently I pulled apart
        The brands and killed the fire.

And never did the blossoms of success
Within my hope's enchanted garden bloom,
And my fair beacon-light of happiness
        Is sunk in gloom.

Faithless Belovèd, many friends are Thine ;
So many love and have been loved by Thee,
They give their hearts, what carest Thou for mine ?
        What need hast Thou of me ?

XXX

O Rival, snatch not from my lips away
The cup that holds the wine of my delight;
The mirror of my joy turns cold and grey,
Darkened before my sight.

As through the gloom the radiant sun above
Comes brightening the world, and shades depart,
So do I burnish with the oil of love
The rust from off my heart.

I vainly stretch imploring hands that long
To touch Hope's gleaming garment as she flies;
Though my desire may fail, yet Hope is strong
And keen, and never dies.

When on the cup that held the drink divine
Of last night's feast the light of morning falls,
The joy of night, the magic of the wine,
The goblet's sight recalls.

Like thee, O Ferhad, in my loneliness
Toiling upon the mountains I have been,
But never drank the sherbet of success,
Sweet as thy lips, Shirin.

Mortals we are, and, fashioned thus of earth,
Vain, Makhfi, is this world in which we trust,
Dust is the rank of kings, the pride of birth,
    Yea, thou thyself art dust.

XXXI

DOWN in the dust and sunken in disgrace
  My honour lies for all the world to see,
But why should I bear shame upon my face?
  What is the honour of the world to me?

Although the times on my unhappy head
  Have heaped the burdens I can hardly bear,
I have not wept; I smile in pride instead;
  Upon my brow are graved no lines of care.

For many years hath sorrow dwelt with me,
  Yet I repine not, and so fiercely wage
My war against despair, it turns to flee—
  I am the Rustum of this later age.

Though callous Fate upon me vengeance wreak,
  O breezes blowing from the heavens above
Bring unto me what I, like Yaqub, seek—
  The perfume of the garments of my Love.

XXXII

Hasten, O Sáki, bring
The wine that it may grant its quickening
To my dead heart, and to the withered flowers
Come like the showers
That give the resurrection of the spring.

What weary days
Are these, that never in the perfumed ways
The bulbul sings among the cypress trees;
Only the morning breeze
Finds entrance there, and with the roses plays.

Masiha, thou canst heal,
Thou wise Physician, hear our heart's appeal!
Give us the bitter draught to cure our grief,
And grant relief;
Blame not the shrinking from thy cup we feel.

Glimmer not, pearly dawn,
Let not the veil of night be yet withdrawn;
I long to send, with arrows of my sighs,
Unto the skies
My eager prayers before the night be gone.

I craved release
From griefs that burn and pains that never cease,
But all my cries to Heaven were empty breath;
Not even Death
Coming at last, could give my spirit peace.

If, on the Judgment Day,
Grieving for my transgressions, I shall pray
For mercy for the evil I have done,
O Self-Existent One,
Grant that my tears shall wash the sin away.

O Makhfi, for thy fate
Be not thou fearful nor disconsolate;
Higher, upon the Day of Reckoning,
Faquir than king,
There shall be then none lowly and none great.

XXXIII

CAST not, Belovéd, on me
Such angry looks from thy narcissus eyes,
Already conquered by their sorcery
Before thy feet my heart a captive lies.

Knotted within my heart,
The very chords that answered to thy touch,
My heart-strings at thy presence thrill and start,
For I have sighed and have lamented much.

O ye who sleep in peace,
You know not of the troubles Love can send,
The days whose tribulations never cease,
The weary nights that drag without an end.

Where, then, does Mecca lie ?
Here is the Kiblah where I make my prayer :
Tell me the physic for my malady—
The anodyne for grief is everywhere.

O Love, where dost thou lead,
Upon what travel fares our caravan ?
By Hedjaz desert shall thy footsteps speed,
The longest journey since the world began.

So poor, indeed, my fate,
Never to me did Love his secrets tell
As to those others, high and fortunate,
Who near his inmost shrine for ever dwell.

XXXIV

WHY should we but in the assembly pray ?
  Only when friends are gathered call for wine ?
Lo, I have done with this hypocrisy,
  And ever pray and drink the cup divine.

The fountain of my spirit has run dry,
  So that in tears no more my sorrow flows,
Mute is the heart that wailed continually,
  Silent the bulbul in the garden-close.

Here, as we tread the pilgrim's way, we find
  The torch of inspiration like a fire,
Men see it not, so dull they are and blind,
  They yearn not for the garments of desire.

To each was given on the Creation-day
  His fitting portion, his appointed share,
Why should'st thou then demand from destiny
  More joy than others have, less pain to bear ?

O Makhfi, for thy counsel all have come,
  Their secrets thou hast kept concealed, apart,
But why should'st thou, who for their sakes art
    dumb,
  Tell shamelessly the secrets of thy heart ?

XXXV

How long upon this soul that dwells in pain
Thy vengeance, O Tormentor, shalt thou pour ?
Could I the Land of Love in peace attain,
Thy poisoned sting should torture me no more.

No unguent salves these wounds upon my heart,
The diamond lancet's healing pang I crave,
So keen my pain I tear my scars apart,
Come with thy kindly cruelty, and save !

From out my keeping has my heart been reft,
Why, let it go then : wherefore should I weep ?
Over the empty hut a faquir left
No watchman comes his careful guard to keep.

Hearken, the time of parting sounds for thee.
How long, O Makhfi, wavering like the fire,
A Kafir shall thy restless spirit be,
Blown like a flame, tormented by desire ?

XXXVI

How hard to read, O Soul,
The riddle of life here and life beyond!
As hard as in the pearl to pierce a hole
Without the needle-point of diamond.

Chide not that 'mongst the flowers
The bulbul doth ecstatically sing;
His passion, yea and his delight, are ours,
Along the garden paths meandering.

We, by our pain made brave,
Seek not despair nor hope; neither outlast
Their little day. We take but what Fate gave,
Not as Zuleikha, brooding o'er the past.

O careless ones, in vain
The treasure of your life has passed away,
Heedless that nothing of your years remain,
You talk like children of another day.

How vain the tears you weep!
Your sorrow fruitless, your remorse too late;
The threshold with your lashes wherefore sweep,
When, Makhfi, see, the shrine is desolate?

XXXVII

When thou unveil'st thy shining countenance,
Burnt are my lashes by thy lightning glance,
And all the night I passionately weep
While o'er my heart tempests of longing sweep ;
And if I see it not, desiring it,
My heart is darkened like a lamp unlit.

I have no hope, no comfort, anywhere,
Caught by the fluttering tresses of thy hair.

No flower can open in my garden bed
Until my heart's blood dyes its petals red.

Sing softly of thy love, or silent be,
O Makhfi, lest the Hunter secretly
Shall come and hear thy voice, and capture thee.

XXXVIII

The love of Thee the bulbul sings,
The moth that burns its silken wings
    Thy love has drawn into the fire,
    And, see, the wine of Thy desire—
On every goblet's lip it clings.

No ease, no respite anywhere
Is now for me, for in Thy snare
    Blindly or willingly I fall,
    No liberty have I at all,
Bound by the fetters of Thy hair.

So many tears mine eyes have shed,
Such streams of blood my heart has bled,
    That now mine eyes can weep no more,
    Nor can the failing fountains pour,
For dry the source from which they fed.

Thou, Makhfi, in the burning fire
Of love and unassuaged desire
    Tossing in wild remorse, shalt dwell;
    Love's secrets weakly didst thou tell,
So thou shalt pay with penance dire.

XXXIX

NOT fierce enough, O moth, the flame to burn
those yearning wings of thine,
Not bright enough the torch of love within our
palace halls to shine.
Mine eyes have scattered pearls of tears, no
consolation did they gain;
The matchless jewel of my soul is given away,
and all in vain;
Long is my bitter tale of grief, of separation
from my Friend,
Unfinished is it even yet, although my life has
reached its end:
Useless, O Saki, is thy cup, no wine of comfort
flows for me
Who drink alone the wine of blood; to others
give thy remedy:
Tale after tale of love is told, linked all together
like a chain.
The fetters hold my heavy heart, of liberty I
dream in vain:
Under the angry storms of death my boat of
life has foundered deep,
My house is fallen, round its dust winds of anni-
hilation sweep.

Yet, Makhfi, if within thy heart the flame of
heavenly love arise,
Thy lonely desert shall be fair as garden groves
of Paradise.

XL

IF from the spot upon my heart the veil
Should fall, and all the world should know my
tale,
How would the roses burn with envious light
Knowing themselves less bright!

Though all the day the leaping fire of sighs
May from my fast-consuming heart arise,
Winds of mischance so blow and scatter it,
My torch is not yet lit.

I leave the world, and to the woods I fly,
But in the forest hunted still am I;
I seek the silence of the lake and hill,
But Love pursues me still.

The malady of Love has turned my brain,
For all my life I have abode with pain;
Then why should I from sorrow seek to flee?
Sorrow is kin to me.

Here in the dwelling of unhappiness,
My silent, desolate sorrow I possess;
For how can shining love with me remain
Within this house of pain?

Behold the pages of my book of life!
Blotted its record, black with sin and strife,
As if the woe of all the world should be
Ever pursuing me.

O Makhfi, from this goblet thou shalt gain
No exaltation, no surcease from pain;
For tears of blood that flow from eyes grown dim
Fill it unto the brim.

XLI

Thou bringest never, long-lost happiness,
To still my heart's distress
The remedy I crave. Why to the crowd
Should I thus voice aloud
My sadness, drawing scorn upon my name,
Telling the world my shame?
If in the close-hung darkness of the night
There shine no thread of light,
What matter? Though no torches flame for me,
My sorrowing heart can see
Illumined by the fire of grief it bears.
Why tangled in the cares
Of worldly hopes, O heart unsatisfied,
Restless wilt thou abide,
Seeking those things that thou shalt never gain?
Help askest thou in vain
From useless friends, and far into the skies
Peace like the Phœnix flies.
Behold, no herb of sweet content has grown;
For we have only sown
In far-off springs the seeds of our disgrace.
How could we bear to face
The direful Judgment Day, did we not bring
Our idol, witnessing

That by this Kafir worship which we give
We true believers live?
Upon the sea of bliss our boat is set,
But comfort comes not yet;
Over the soul waves of the tempest rise
Menacing to the skies.

So weary, Makhfi, are thine eyes with tears,
Darkened the world appears,
Nor can they tell, by grief and watching worn,
The rosebud from the thorn.

XLII

O Self-Existent, give
Unto Thy faithful ones their heart's desire,
And visit not with Thy consuming fire
O'er-burdened souls, too sorrowful to live.

No longer can I bear
The separation and the bitter grief;
Afflicted am I—grant my soul relief!
Weary and broken—look on my despair!

O Thou, whose praise we tell,
Sever the tyrant bonds, give to the slave
His freedom, save him, Lord, as Thou did'st save
Yusuf, the Moon of Canaan, from the well!

My tears fail, for they must;
The spring that fed their fountains has run dry;
Give me Thy peace, O Lord; for what am I?
Only a handful of afflicted dust.

But flowers of hope return
To bloom within my garden of desire,
For God can call even from flames of fire
Tulips like torches to arise and burn.

XLIII

On my tormented heart appears
  Another deep and glowing stain,
Again there dawns my day of tears
  Of misery, of weary pain.

So much of mine own blood I shed,
  So long the journeys I have done,
So difficult the path I tread,
  To catch the garment of the sun!

New balm within my heart is borne,
  New lightnings from my glance arise,
Why then your anger, and the scorn
  Flashing from your narcissus eyes?

Out of my heart you reft away
  The life, my heart from out its place
You ravished, and I can but pray—
  O lift the veil that hides your face!

XLIV

Long, long am I denied
The vision of thy face, for o'er it flows
The musky darkness of thy waving hair,
As though a temple-curtain should enclose
The Kaaba, and our hearts, unsatisfied,
Could never see it there.

O Reason, that can speed
A runner in the valley of desire,
We need not strength like thine, for we possess
A remedy to cure us when we tire;
The thorns and brambles are the salves we need
For pain and weariness.

Night after endless night
I sat in lonely grief remembering thee;
Tears fell into my heart disconsolate.
How long have I, in striving to be free,
Broken my bleeding nails, but never quite
Untied the knot of fate!

Lo, where the feast was spread,
What better could I offer to my guest
Than wine and music when we revelled long ?
Of all the wines the wine of tears was best,
One song of sorrow to another led,
Making continual song.

Thou shalt attain success,
O happy lover, walking on the height ;
Thy shadow greater shall be evermore
Than King Jamshid's, and plumes and pinions bright
As hath the Phœnix, shall thy soul possess,
Arrogantly to soar.

By sorrow crucified,
A true believer lost his life for thee,
And yet did not attain what I attain :
This new delight which is bestowed on me
Even the friends who travelled by my side
Could never know nor gain.

Red with its fount of tears
Thy rosy face doth like a tulip show,
To tell what dreams within thy heart arise.
My tears have washed with their unceasing flow,
The magic cup wherein the world appears
Displayed before mine eyes.

Stronger my love shall grow:
Bearing the bonds of sorrow for thy sake,
More patient and more proud my heart shall be,
Like the imprisoned bird who tries to make
His cage a garden, though his wild heart know
He never shall be free.

Behold Love's path—it seems
So long, O Makhfi; but be strong to tread
Its toilsome way, and come, nor look behind;
The temple where thou canst bow down thy head,
The idol fairer than thy fairest dreams,
Thou shalt desire, and find.

XLV

No way of joy and ease is mine to tread,
The road of shame and madness joyfully I choose instead;
And from my heart such streams of blood shall pour
Upon the Day of Judgment, that the Desert crimsoned o'er
Shall all the rosy hues of heaven outvie,
And Paradise be darkened, envious of its flaming dye.
If, penitent, I shed one tear of shame,
Then shall be cleansed the follies and the sins that stained my name;
For God shall show compassion in that day,
My record of transgressions shall be wholly swept away.
The tree of World's Desire has set its roots
Deep planted in the darkness; sin and shame its bitter fruits;
Then barter not the wealth contentment brings
For all the wide dominions of a thousand mighty kings.

If from my heart I loose my heavy sighs
Black whirling from the Desert shall the blinding dust arise.

Though, Makhfi, God shall pardon at the last,
The Skirt of Intercession hold within thy fingers fast.

XLVI

O GIVE me, friends, your care,
Lest in my madness loudly I proclaim
The secrets of the Lord, that all may know.
Like wax I melt within Love's eager flame,
But in my breast a heart of stone I bear,
Mocking its glow.

Down unto death I went,
The Heavens upon me showered their cruel blows.
Pity me, O ye Chosen Ones of God!
O Enemy, when shall I gain repose,
How long shall I groan under chastisement,
Wince 'neath the rod?

How darkened is my fame!
Extravagantly have I spent my store,
And empty-handed in the market stand;
A dervish am I, and can give no more,
No emperor, with glory round my name
And lavish hand.

Foundered my boat of life;
Vainly upon the ocean of despair
I ventured out, seeking the tranquil shore
And the Beloved. No farther can I dare—
I bow to Fate, I turn me from the strife,
I scheme no more.

The time of spring is past,
The rose-leaves in the garden drift apart,
Among the trees the bulbul sings no more.
How long, O madness, shalt thou hold my heart?
How long, O exaltation, shalt thou last
Now spring is o'er?

How uselessly is spent
And cast away the treasure of my life,
In bitter separation from my Friend!
Surely, O cruel Heavens, might now my strife
My grief, my pain, my weary discontent,
Attain the end!

O King, O Teacher, see—
E'en in the tale of Alexander's fate,
Most fortunate of mortals, thou canst read
Of Dara, broken and disconsolate;
Yea, sorrowful his shadowed history
Appears indeed.

Upon the feasting day
Friends joyfully in the assembly meet,
But Makhfi in the lane of sorrow goes
Slowly and loth, with melancholy feet,
No rest, no ease, no peace upon the way,
The faquir knows.

XLVII

UNTO the garden floats the wandering air
To tell the roses that are waiting there
The tidings of thy coming; soft and sweet
Their petals open as they kiss thy feet.

If from thy moon-like face the veil arise,
No more will Yusuf turn regretful eyes
Homeward to Canaan: he will only see
Thy face, and offer all his love to thee.

No remedy can heal the heart's distress
Except the vision of thy loveliness.
Here, suffering souls, the solace that you need!
Tear not your wounds, no longer make them
bleed.

How difficult the hunted deer to find,
Although his scent be left upon the wind;
How hard to reach thee, though thine every tress
Breathes musk of Khotan through the wilderness!

O happy Makhfi! fortunate thy day!
For thou at the Belovèd's feet may lay
Thy song in homage; happier still, if thou
Sing rapturously evermore as now!

XLVIII

So tyrannous thine eyes,
Even the morning breeze is hot with wrath,
No soft assuagement in its breath it hath,
It only faints and dies.

Like Khizr, strong and fair,
Whose soul is steeped in the immortal spring,
The well of life, thou shalt be worshipping
With holy words of prayer.

Born to the Khalif's place,
None other heired such high estate as thine,
Thou hast the beauty that is all divine,
Fairer than peri's grace.

From hope I turned in hate;
No further now false hope can cozen me.
I know the cruel Heavens conspired with thee
To darken thus my fate.

Makhfi, thy life flows fast,
The days from out thy hand drop evermore;
O turn no weary traveller from thy door,
Give him what cheer thou hast.

XLIX

Let not thy curl, whose loveliness
Maddens the world, bring new distress
Upon thy lovers, floating free,
Tossed by the wind, that all may see
And fall beneath thy sorcery.

Let not the valley of thy love
A place of bitter torment prove
For dolorous souls, already worn
By all the penance they have borne,
Betrayed by love, and left forlorn.

No flower, no nightingale am I,
So from the garden mournfully
I go. O breezes, free to stray,
Back to her garden find your way,
And greeting to my Love convey.

Exiled and driven from thee I pass
Upon my journey; like the grass
And patient reeds I bend and shake,
As my despairing road I take,
Leaving the body for thy sake.

Before the soul who understands
Be silent: in the desert sands
He learnt his lore. Break not the rest
Of the afflicted and oppressed
With poisoned arrows in his breast.

L

O MIGHT I have as surma for mine eyes
The dust that on her happy threshold lies,
And there might waiting kneel to kiss at last
Her feet like those of angels fluttering past!
My soul has girt around it suffering
And wears it as the garment that a king
Gives to his servant, decking him with pride.
O Enemy that waitest by my side,
How long shall I be bent beneath thy rod,
And walk the path of pain my friends have trod?
The storm sweeps round my house, its ramparts fail,
Its deep foundations sway before the gale.
I am a bird, who, flying home to rest,
Finds that the waters have o'erwhelmed his nest.

Sell not the jewel of thy soul so cheap,
No friends can help thy heart its wealth to keep.

O King of all the roses, be thou kind
Unto the bulbul, whose unquiet mind
Makes him a mad faquir in loving thee;
For even kings who ride in majesty

Will stop their chariots e'er a faquir stir.
Blessèd is Makhfi: God has given to her
The pearl of words, jewel of song divine,
Fairer than spoils of ocean or of mine.

NOTES

Alexander: in Persian poetry the type of the most fortunate one, as is Darius of the most unfortunate.

Ayub: Job.

Diwan: a Diwan consists of a series of groups of ghazals (*q.v.*), the first collection rhyming with the first letter of the alphabet, the second with the second, and so on through the alphabet.

Ferhad: a lover famous in Eastern story. He loved Shirin (the sweet one), who was the wife of King Khosru, about the end of the sixth century. He was a sculptor, and renowned throughout Persia. The King, fearing his rivalry, tried to divert his mind from his passion, and sought to find for him some impossible task. As Shirin had demanded a "river of milk," he was bidden to clear away the rocks obstructing the passage of the great mountain of Beysitoun, and to cause the rivers on the opposite sides of the mountain to join. Ferhad agreed on condition that, if he were successful, Shirin should be given to him. For years he laboured, and carved out wonderful caverns, which can be seen to this day; and the Joui-shir (stream of milk) still flows from the mountain between Hamadân and Hulwân. Only a few days' work remained to be done, when the King heard reports that the project was succeeding: he thereupon sent a messenger to tell Ferhad that Shirin was dead. On hearing this, Ferhad died, some say by killing himself with his axe, others say by throwing himself over a precipice.

Ghazal, or *gazel*: a form of verse written in a succession of couplets. The first two lines rhyme, and of the succeeding couplets the first line is unrhymed, the second rhymes with the first couplet, and so on, throughout the poem; so that, in the whole poem, all the words which rhyme, rhyme with one another. When this form of verse consists of only four lines, it is called a *Rubai*. The length of a ghazal varies, but it is not supposed to be longer than eighteen couplets. Often the couplets within a ghazal have no apparent connection, and are complete in themselves. The last couplet usually contains the name of the poet.

Hatim, or *Hatim Tai:* an Arabian chief famed for his generosity: he never refused a request. He was born in Yemen, in Arabia Felix, in pre-Musulman times. Some one asked for his head, and he gave it, and so died.

Hedjaz: the greatest desert in Arabia; along its length pass the principal caravan routes.

Jamshid: the type of the magnificent king. He belonged to the mythical Peshdadian dynasty, and flourished about 800 B.C. He was reputed to be the builder of Persepolis. His reign was a kind of golden age, when sickness and death were unknown. The angel Siroush descended from Heaven to visit him, and left him a robe and an enchanted girdle. He was gifted, like Moses, with a ray of divine light; so that once, when he was descending Mount Alborz, the crowd imagined that there were two suns in the world. His ring and throne had magic powers: when he looked into his seven-ringed goblet he could see what was passing in all the worlds. But pride came into his heart, and he forgot God; his subjects revolted against him and drove him from his kingdom; and he roamed the earth an outcast for a hundred years. He repented, and was restored, with undiminished youth, to his kingdom and power.

Kaaba: the chief sanctuary of Mecca, the holy city of the Musulmans. The Kaaba was revered before the time of Muhammad, and was then a rude stone building; its name came from a word meaning an astralagus, or die, because of its roughly cubical shape. It has been several times rebuilt, but the old form has been preserved except in secondary details. Into its wall is built an ancient black stone, possibly an aerolite, said to have been given by the angel Gabriel to Abraham.

Kafir: an unbeliever; one who is not a Musulman.

Kaikobad: a Sultan of the Seljukian dynasty, renowned not only for his successful wars, but as a great builder of palaces.

Kerbela : the place of the massacre of Hussain, the grandson of the Prophet, and his children, by the Ommeyyades. It is situated in Mesopotamia, near the western bank of the Tigris, twenty-eight miles from the ruins of Babylon. It is a great place of pilgrimage for the Shiahs, who hold that the spiritual leadership of Islam devolved upon Ali; the son-in-law of Muhammad, and his descendants. The tomb of Hussain is in a large mosque; and each year two hundred thousand pilgrims from all parts of the Musulman world visit it, sometimes carrying the bones of their ancestors to be buried there. The story of the death of Hussain is annually read, and sometimes enacted as a miracle-play, in Shiah communities, with much wailing and sorrow, on the tenth day of the Mohurrum celebrations.

Khizr : the angel-guardian of the spring of immortality.

Kiblah : the direction in which Mecca lies, indicated by the mehrab, or niche, in the wall of a mosque, to which the worshippers turn in prayer.

Leila and *Majnun :* the heroine and hero of the celebrated Arabian love-story told by many poets, of whom the most famous are Jami, Nizami, and Hatifi. Kaïs was the son of an Arabian chief, but, madly loving Leila, the daughter of a neighbouring chief, he was called Majnun, or the mad one. Leila was married to a more powerful suitor, and Majnun wandered for years in the desert, where he taught the secrets of love to the birds and beasts.

Mahmoud : the praised one, a name of the Prophet.

Majnun : the lover of Leila (*q.v.*).

Makhfi : the hidden one.

Mansur : Mansur al-Hallaj, a Persian saint of the ninth century, who was crucified at Baghdad for declaring that he was one with God.

Masiha : Messiah. Jesus is known in Musulman tradition as the Healer.

Phœnix : a fabulous bird of great size and beauty, habitually dwelling in the Caucasus Mountains, but appearing at very rare intervals. If it spreads its wings over the head of a man, he becomes a king. It was supposed to live for seventeen hundred years, and only one existed in the world at a time.

Rustum: son of Zal, Prince of Seistan: a traditional hero of Persia, famous for his indomitable strength and bravery. He conquered the Dives, or evil spirits, and performed other miraculous deeds, comparable to the labours of Hercules. He is the hero of the *Shah-Nameh* of Firdausi.

Saki: the cupbearer.

Shirin: the beloved of Ferhad (*q.v.*). The name means "sweet."

Suleiman: King Solomon; in Musulman legend lord over angels and demons, of great wisdom and power, understanding the language, not only of all men, but of the beasts and birds. His power lay in his possessing the seal with the name of God.

Surma: kohl, or collyrium, a black powder used in Egypt and the East for darkening the eyelids and thus giving lustre to the eyes.

Turks: the Turcomans from Turkestan, who ravaged Central Asia from Persia to India and east to China, the Great Wall of which was built as a protection against them.

Yaqub: Jacob, who in Musulman tradition became blind by weeping for the loss of his son Joseph, who had been sold by his brothers as a slave into Egypt; he regained his sight when he smelt the garment of his son which had been brought to him.

Yusuf: Joseph, who is regarded as of superhuman loveliness, surrounded by celestial light, the emblem of divine perfection. He possessed nine-tenths of the beauty allotted to the whole world.

Zuleikha: daughter of Taimus, King of Mauretania. In a dream she saw and fell in love with the image of Yusuf; she was not told his name, but only that his abode was Egypt. She went to Memphis to marry Asiz Potiphar, the Grand Vizier of Pharaoh, imagining her future husband was the vision of her dream. Yusuf was sold as a slave, and was purchased by her; but, being warned by the angel Gabriel in the likeness of his father Jacob, he fled from her. She is represented as always brooding over her lost happiness.

Printed by Hazell, Watson & Viney, Ld., London and Aylesbury.